Tongan traditions in brief

Lectures by Professor Semisi Pone

SEMISI PONE
BSc, MSc (Hons)

Copyright © Rainbow Enterprises 2017

Publisher: Rainbow Enterprises 2017

ISBN: 978-1-98-851116 -0

Distributor: Rainbow Enterprises

Email: rainbowenterprises7@gmail.com

Revised Version, Second Edition

Dedication

**This ebook is dedicated to all my Tongan relatives,
ancestors, uncles and aunts who gave me a good
'grounding' in the Tongan Culture and Customs.**

INTRODUCTION

This book is a collection of lectures by myself in the 'School of Tongan Traditions and Dance' on our page in Facebook.

It was a decision of the Board of Trustees, which I have finally 'actioned' as Chief Executive of the Trust. The 'Project Revival Charity Trust (Inc), was established through a Deed of Trust in New Zealand in June 2013. The establishment of the school was part of its principles and purposes. It has begun through these lectures until such time funding and resources allow for premises, staff and a curriculum to be set up.

I am the Acting Chair and Professor until we find somebody to takeover this position, which is currently advertised, of Chair of the School and Professor of Tongan traditions and Dance. I include my experience here for the benefit of the reader.

The objective of these lectures is to start the activities of the school as planned by the

Board of Trustees and also to plan the establishment of premises, staff and curriculum for the school for disadvantaged Tongan youth or anyone interested in Tongan traditions and dance, in New Zealand and throughout the world.

Most Tongan kids born overseas in New Zealand, Australia and the United States do not speak Tongan or know much about the culture of their country of origin. It is the idea of the school to provide this information for them. Most parents born in Tonga speak in Tongan and know about the culture but they sometimes are too busy to teach the kids.

That is why the school is 24/7, 365-366 days a year so the information is available to all Tongan kids, and their parents, in New Zealand and throughout the world.

Malo ʻaupito

Acting Professor Semisi Pule also known as Semisi Pule Pone.

1. THE SCHOOL OF TONGAN TRADITIONS AND DANCE

The Board of Trustees has approved, in the last agenda (August, 2015), previous plans for a Chair of the School. This person will be responsible for future operations of the School. The Chair will have the title 'Professor of Tongan Traditions and Dance'. It will be a contract, but still volunteer position. A person, preferably a retired professor/teacher in this area, will be invited to be the Chair and be responsible for developing the School Curriculum and finding funds for the school premises and so on. This position will be responsible to the Chief Executive in implementing and carrying out his/her tasks as described in the 'Job Description'.

Once the 'Chair' or 'Professor' is on board we can formalize the school with its curriculum, activities and hopefully find premises for the commercial office of the school and the trust.

Nominations can be made to the 'Chief Executive' by email on rainbowenterprises7@gmail.com. If you know somebody who will be suitable for this position send me a note.

2. BACKGROUND OF THE CHIEF EXECUTIVE, ACTING PROFESSOR.

NAME : **Semisi Pule a.k.a Semisi Pule Pone**

TITLE: **Acting Professor, Tongan Traditions and Dance**

QUALIFICATION

Bachelor of Science (1985), Master of Science (Honours) (1989), Auckland University, NEW ZEALAND.

WORK EXPERIENCE

-    6 years (1985-1992) MAFF, Tonga as Plant Pathologist, Senior Plant Virologist, Secretary of the Quarantine, Pesticide Committees. Post entry quarantine.

-    Lecturer in Biology and Ecology at 'Atenisi University (1991)

-    Fellow in Tissue Culture at the University of the South Pacific, Alafua Campus, Samoa (1992-1993).

-    Head of the Plant Protection Service, Plant Protection Advisor, Co-ordinator of the Plant Protection Service, South Pacific Commission, Suva, Fiji (1993-1996)

-    Acting Chief Executive of the Pacific Plant Protection Organization (1995-1996)

-    7 years appointed member of FAO, Rome, United Nations expert committee on Biosecurity

-    Member or RPPO technical consultations, Rome, FAO-UN (1993-1996)

MANAGEMENT EXPERIENCE

-    Manager of the $5 million SPC/EU Plant Protection in the Pacific project (1993-1996).

-    Co-ordinator of the SPC Plant Protection Service (1993-1996).

-    Acting Chief Executive of the Pacific Plant Protection Organization (1995-1996)

-    Co-ordinator/Secretary/Chief Executive of the Project Revival Charity Trust (Inc) (2013-present).

WRITING EXPERIENCE

-    Columnist for the Matangi Tonga magazine, 1989-1991

-    Author of more than 100 books, ebooks and pdf books on sale in NZ and more than 200 countries worldwide.

EXPERIENCE ON TONGAN TRADITIONS AND DANCE

- 40 years learning traditions and dance from family, relatives, elders and professionals.

- Song/Tongan/English composer.

Tongan compositions so far include;

1. Hinaola 2. 'Isa he Manatu 3. 'Angelo sei 'o e Ngoue (available from Youtube)

English compositions so far; 1. Dope dealers 2. Kid in Town 3. Twinkle in your eye (available from Youtube)

THE SC HOOL OF TONGAN TRADITIONS AND DANCE

This idea is to encourage Tongan kids or kids of Tongan origin who live outside Tonga or in any country in the world to learn something about their country of origin and their poetry/songs and dance. There are more than twice the population in Tonga or 200,000+ Tongans or part Tongans that live outside Tonga. So it is important to start this

conversation for all to share.
I will start with my own compositions and we will continue to some of Queen Salote's songs and others. It is said that Queen Salote composed more than 300 songs so it will be interesting to count all of them.
These are some of the traditional/cultural topics that we will discuss.

1. Faka'apa'apa or respect in its many forms
2. Tukufakaholo or heritage in its many forms

We can add more as we go along and everyone is welcome to contribute.

Lecture 1 - Faka'apa'apa or respect

- There are many forms of 'faka'apa'apa' in Tongan society. Faka'apa'apa for 1. parents 2. older siblings/cousins 3. sisters/female cousins 4. village/family elders 5. Chiefs 6. Government officials 7. King 8. Uncles and Aunties

<u>Faka'apa'apa or respect for parents</u> is based on many premises.
(i) they are the providers for the family

(ii) they are the elders of the family (iii) they are the 'creators' of the family (iv) they are the protectors of the family (v) they are the leaders of the family (vi) they are the administrators of the family (vii) they are the counselors/disciplinarians (viii) religious figureheads in the family. There are more, but lets discuss those.

This is very straight forward. Faka'apa'apa or respect that Tongan children have for their parents are learned and mostly based on these premises or reasons.

(i) Providers - children learn from an early age that Mum and Dad provide everything for them. Food, shelter, clothes, medicine, comfort, love, affection, pride, siblings, relatives and extended family; in fact Mum and Dad provide the whole world in the child's eyes.

(ii) As elders of the family, Mum and Dad are the administrators, counselors, disciplinarians, figureheads and leaders of the family. The kids feel they will be totally lost without Mum and Dad and rely/trust them completely in everything they do. Although they don't know how at an early age, but Tongan kids know that it was Mum and Dad that brought them into this world.

<u>Faka'apa'apa or respect for older siblings</u> and cousins. In Tongan culture the oldest male child is the future head of the extended family, or 'ulumotu'a, and they are trained from a young age for that responsibility. All the younger siblings, both male and female, will obey the oldest male in all things to do with the family as a sign of 'faka'apa'apa' for his leadership role. If there is no male then the oldest female assumes this role or a male cousin of the oldest uncle or auntie on the father's side of the family. Sometimes the younger brothers assume this leadership role if the oldest is absent or unable to do his duty.

<u>Faka'apa'apa or respect for sisters</u> and female cousins is totally different. In Tongan culture, the brother-sister relationship is taboo. They must not sleep in the same room, share the same clothes, plate, talk to each other and so on in the old days. They lived in different houses. The sister is also known as the 'fahu' to the brother's children. The 'fahu' is the most chiefly person or highest ranked person in the family and she is entitled to take anything from her brother's family. The

brother's descendants will always be inferior to the sisters descendants. This kind of 'faka'apa'apa' also works at the highest level of ancient Tongan society....with the highest ranked person, a female, called the 'Tamaha'. She is usually the female child of a 'Female Tu'i Tonga/King and another King usually one from a special area.

<u>Faka'apa'apa for female cousins</u> works also in the same way but much less taboo and the ranks in terms of their parents (brother/sister) come into play. In Tongan society, some second cousins usually marry especially the Royals. Commoners practice the brother-sister taboo with even 3rd and 4th cousins.

<u>Faka'apa'apa or respect for village or extended family elders</u>....or the Church Minister....or village church leaders. There is always a special kind of   'faka'apa'apa' reserved for the elders of the village who are also extended family members, especially in events like courtship, weddings, funerals. In most courtships, the male child who likes a female in the village will go and tell his uncle and other elders in the 'kainga' or extended family

and they will take another elder who is called a 'matapule' or family spokesperson....and even the 'faifekau' or church minister. They will take some kava and maybe some mats and yams and a pig to do the 'lea'....this means the boy will ask (lea...to speak) the girl to marry him in the traditional way. They all go to the girl's house to do the 'lea mali' (asking for her hand in marriage).

They may have known each other for a while. Sometimes there are several 'faikava' or kava ceremony before the 'lea'. This kind of role reserves elders 'faka'apa'apa' for those purposes. It is different in a funeral...which is controlled by the eldest in the family or 'ulumotu'a' who was trained for that ...and other duties like the family weddings, birthdays or anything that requires decision making. The 'ulumotu'a' or 'head of the extended family' plays the lead role in all family decision making and activities. In most of the family gatherings in the villages, the Church Minister or elder in the church plays an important role ....because all Tongan extended family gatherings start with prayers and end with prayers or 'lotu'.

<u>Faka'apa'apa or respect for Chiefs</u> - Each village in Tonga has its own Chief or caretaker who looks after the land and the people for the King, except some villages or land which are Government property. There are jobs that the Chief does and there is also certain protocols to be followed when the villagers want to see the Chief about something. The faka'apa'apa for the Chiefs is through his traditional authority and is usually shown through the 'fatongia'. Fatongia is a word that applies to all things to do with people's love of their family, relatives, village, Chief, Government and King. It is their feeling that...... it is their duty to do something. The 'fatongia' includes providing pigs, kava, yams and mats and so on for the Chief's instalment.....then there are regular duties or 'fatongia' that the Chief must perform for the King and Government. The people of the village show their respect through their 'fatongia' by providing everything the Chief needs to meet his obligations including in some cases...cash.

The Chief reciprocates by distributing food, goods and land to his relatives, these (except the land) are usually from occasions like the

recent coronation of the King in July 2015, for example.
The Chief also presides over many of the village 'fono' or meetings and looks after all the affairs of the village.

Faka'apa'apa or respect for the King - In Tongan society, the King is the Head of the Government and Paramount Chief. In ancient times there were other people who were considered even more sacred than the King like the 'Tamaha' mentioned before. But in present day Tonga, the King is the Head of State. The King, according to folklore and probably in the constitution, owns all the land in Tonga. His 33 Lords/Nobles look after the estates for the King. They administer them and ensure that the distribution of land according to the constitution is fair to all their village subjects.

The King is also the Paramount Chief of the country, so he holds the administrative 'Head of State' and also the traditional authority as 'Paramount Chief'. The 'taumafa kava' or the kava ceremony instals him as Paramount

Chief occupying the head of the kava circle or Olovaha. He is also crowned in the biggest Church in Tonga as the Head of State or King. The 'faka'apa'apa' or respect for the King is also shown through the 'fatongia' in its various forms at various levels of Tongan society from the Lords/Nobles, Government Officials down to the commoners in the villages.

These 'fatongia' include; 1. services to King and Country 2. traditional obligations such as provision of pigs and kava to the 'fakapangai' or various kava ceremonies to instal Chiefs and Kings. 3. 'A'ahi or visits by various groups, churches, villages, Ha'a (group of Chiefs) and so on...during special occasions such as funerals, weddings, Christmas and New Year

The 'fatongia' is a show of the subjects 'love and respect for the King' or the Lords/Nobles when such occasions like the 'fakapangai' require them to provide the necessities.

There are also matters to do within the Royal Family itself that demands respect or 'faka'apa'apa for the King.

<u>Faka'apa'apa or respect between husband and wife</u>

-    In ancient times a man can have as many wives as he wants especially if you have high rank. Some of the ancient kings were reputed to have more than 200 wives. However, in modern Tonga a man can only have one wife. Unlike ancient times and some countries, it is against the law to marry more than one woman. Polygamy is taboo in modern Tonga.

The man's job is to provide food for the family by working in his farm and growing all the food they need. He also goes fishing to supplement their meals with seafood. If he works for the Government and lives in Nuku'alofa, he probably buy everything they need.

The wife cooks, wash the clothes, clean the house, look after the kids and usually does what the man as the head of the family wants. They respect each other because they know they depend on each other for the smooth operation of the family but more importantly for moral support. This respect is also shown through various forms of tasks, duties and fatongia which cements the relationship.
The extended family also play a role in their

relationship and the respect they have for them depend on how they perform their fatongia which encompasses just about everything they do for each other, the family, the extended family and village.

Lecture 2 - Tukufakaholo

I have touched on some aspects of 'faka'apa'apa' or respect, now I will discuss 'tukufakaholo' or heritage or some points that I think are worth mentioning. First, the kava. Kava (*Piper methysticum*) is a very important plant in Tongan culture. Like alcohol in European culture it is the central and most unifying activity at all levels of Tongan society.....sharing a bowl of kava and some stories in the evenings. Lo'au, one of the legendary figures of Tongan history, is credited with the 'Kava Ceremony'.

This is what Lo'au proposed when the first kava plant was presented with its story (I will include the story of Kava later). This 'laulau' or poem by Lo'au is the original foundation of the Kava Ceremony.

Koe laulau 'o e kava

Ko Kava koe kilia mei Fa'imata
Koe tama 'a Fevanga mo Fefafa
Fahifahi pea mama
Ha tano'a mono anga
Ha pulu mono tata
Ha pelu ke tau'anga
Ha Mu'a ke 'apa'apa
Ha 'Eiki ke Olovaha
Fai'anga 'o e Taumafa Kava

Lo'au is reputed to be a foreigner, probably of Spanish origin. He was said to have a compass or 'jellyfish' tatooed on his hand or palm. You can tell from the laulau that it is kind of 'half caste' in nature. The use of the word...mono...is just like how a European would speak Tongan.

Lo'au also had a compass tatooed on his hand which was peculiar to famous Tongans like Lepuha, for example. They were either sailors marooned in Tonga or spies during the age of colonization around the world. Lo'au is also said to have sailed towards the 'setting sun' and never returned. He probably returned to Europe. He, most likely, got the idea for the Kava Ceremony from the 'alcohol drinking culture' of Europe' or from other islands he visited where kava was shared as a social drink.

Another famous ancient Tongan, Lepuha, was reputed to be popular with women. He would come into a meeting and show any woman present his tattoo of the 'jellyfish' and she would stand up and follow him. The Tongans thought it was a sexual liaison but probably more of 'spy activities' with the tattoo the 'password'. It was the age of colonization and Schouten and Le Maire (1616), Abel Tasman (1643) and Captain James Cook (1777) have visited the Tongan Islands in search of supplies and probably natural resources for Europe and their growing empires around the world.

Tonga does not have any natural resources and, probably, the main reason why the Europeans left them alone. They only came in large numbers to Tonga later when whale and coconut oil were needed for the lamps in British and European homes and streets.

The Story of Kava

There was a couple who lived on the island of 'Eueiki named Fevanga and Fefafa. They had one girl, Kava, who was a leper. During one dry period or drought, there was a visitor to their island. It was said to be one of the Tu'i Tonga. He was hungry and directed the Kalia to be diverted to 'Eueiki for supplies. There was only one edible plant on the whole island, which was a giant taro or kape which grew on the beach. The King's warriors searched the whole island for food and met Fevanga and Fefafa who told them there is one giant taro plant on the beach. They will cook it for the King.

Fevanga went to the beach to bring the giant taro, he found the King sitting with his back to it, so he retreated back to their house and told Fefafa. They cannot tell the King to move so he can harvest the plant, so they killed their daughter Kava and cooked her in a 'umu or earth oven. The King's warriors reported what happened to the King who instructed them not to open the 'umu and promptly left for Tongatapu. After a while Fevanga and Fefafa noticed two plants growing on the mound where the 'umu was.

One day a mouse came and ate the plant at Kava's feet, it staggered around and ate from the plant at Kava's head and ran straight into the bush. They harvested the plants and took them to the King. After they told the King the story, the plant at Kava's feet was called the Kava which was 'kona' or caused the mouse to stagger and the one at her head was called 'to' (sugarcane) which was sweet and caused the mouse to become well again.

Presumably Lo'au was present in the King's court and he prepared the first Kava ceremony which is described in his 'laulau' or poem. It is known to-day as the 'Laulau 'o e Kava' or the 'Poem of Kava'. The traditional 'fono' or food after the Kava ceremony was sugarcane....but now people prefer a roast pig and some yams other food or even beer!.

Tukufakaholo or heritage - Language

I will talk about the language used for different classes of Tongan society namely

King, Lords/Nobles and Commoners or Tu'i, Hou'eiki, Kakai.

Some examples.

Tu'i (King)	Hou'eiki (Lords)	Kakai (Commoners)	English
Taumafa	'ilo	kai, fafa'o	eat
folofola	me'a	lea	speak
mulumulu	takele	kaukau	bath, shower
ha'ele	me'a	lele	walk, run
houhau	tuputamaki	'ita	angry

Commoners were also known as me'avale or the 'stupid ones'. In ancient times the people of high rank were trained in all aspects of Tongan etiquette and everything they need to know about their role in ancient Tongan society. The term 'eiki was used to refer to people of high rank. They are expected to behave like a person of high rank or angafaka'ei'eiki

In most villages the 'me'avale' or 'stupid ones' or commoners are considered untrained, unworthy and are usually killed if they anger or insult a person of higher rank. They are expected to do all the work for the family and village from farming to cooking and menial chores.

During wartime, the Chief and men of high rank (hou'eiki) are considered and trained to be the warriors and protectors of the island or village. The King does not usually get involved in wars but act as the 'command post' from his palace or fort. The 'me'avale'/stupid ones are the ones who carry the necessities of a war....they are the mules. They do all the other work to enable the chiefs/warriors to carry out their duties as protectors/attackers and so on.

In peace time the Chiefs/Kings pleasure themselves with compositions of music, dance and similar leisure activities or building, directing farming, fishing and so on. They act as the supervisors for the me'avale/stupid ones who do the work.
Some of the dances still practiced to-day include the me'e tu'upaki, lakalaka, ma'ulu'ulu, soke, tau-fakaNiua, tau'olunga. You can see a lot of those dances by searching on Youtube.

Some of the dances originate from other islands.

Tukufakaholo also involve the genealogy of Tongan families. Most of the Kings and Lords have well documented genealogies. The me'avale/stupid ones usually have no record of their existence.

James Cocker has done a great job putting together the 'Tuputupu Le Fanua' which is one of the best genealogy records I have seen on line. He has put together the genealogy for the Tu'i Tonga, Tu'i Ha'a Takalaua and Tu'i Kanokupolu. You can read about the genealogy of Tokemoana and other genealogies and a whole lot of other traditions, customs and Tongan proverbs or ancient words on his page.

In Tonga now (2015) there is only 1 King, 33 Lords/Nobles and 100,000 commoners/me'avale.

However, through education the commoners or me'avale are now highly trained with Bachelors, Masters and Doctorates. They are titles (BSc, MSc, PhD) that are highly sought after around the world. The commoners occupy government positions from Prime Minister, Government Ministers down to the lowest level clerks in government and laborers. They are no longer me'avale but are very smart, clever and resourceful members of modern Tongan society. The Chiefs/Lords/Nobles are now relegated to occupy the 'less trained' level of modern Tonga, but still holding on to their traditional authority which is the basis of their wealth.

In ancient times there were many Kings or Tu'i, they include the Tu'i Niua, Tu'i Vava'u, Tu'i Ha'apai, Tu'i Ha'angana, Tu'i Tonga, Tu'i 'Eua, Tu'i 'Afitu, Tu'i Pelehake, Tu'i Lakepa, Tu'i Ha'ateiho, Tu'i Ha'a Takalaua, Tu'i Kanolupolu, Tu'i Ha'a 'Uluakimata and so on. In the Tongan occupied parts of Fiji and Samoa, there were the Tu'i Viti, Tu'i Lau, Tu'i Kadavu, Tu'i Moala, Tu'i Nayau, Tu'i Lakeba, Tu'i Ha'amoa, Tu'i Manu'a and so on.

There were many more Chiefs as well. A Chief's rank is based on his heritage or parent's genealogy. Every man descendant from the Kings was considered a Chief. It was only after the 50 years civil war in Tonga that the number of Chiefs was reduced to 33. The war began in 1799 with the assassination of Tuku'aho, 14th Tu'i Kanokupolu by the Tu'i Vava'u and his warriors....because Tuku'aho had insulted their aunty the 12th Tu'i Kanokupolu, Tupou Moheofo, who is of higher rank.

Taufa'ahau , grandson of Tuku'aho, who was Tu'i Ha'apai, Tu'i Vava'u and later Tu'i Kanokupolu won the war by beating everyone including the 39th and last Tu'i Tonga, Laufilitonga, at Velata in Lifuka. After 900+ years of Tu'i Tonga rule it ended with the death of Laufilitonga in 1865. The Tu'i Tonga was the Paramount Chief of ancient Tonga.

Taufa'ahau established a new government in the Westminster Model, in 1875, with the help of British Missionaries and selected only 33 Chiefs to join in his new government. All other chiefly titles were abolished. Taufa'ahau who was a Christian adopted an English name after the King of England/UK, King George Tupou I. King George Tupou II succeeded Tupou I then Queen Salote Tupou III, then

Taufa'ahau Tupou IV, then King George Tupou V, then King George Tupou VI , the current King.

Land heritage

As mentioned before, all the land in Tonga belong to the King...as stated in Tonga's 'Coat of Arms'....'God and Tonga are my Inheritance'. The first King (King George Tupou I) had conquered all the islands so all the land belong to him.

In an act called the 'foaki' he divided the country into estates which his 33 Lords/Nobles oversee and distributed the land to the people. Some land was left to the Government. Every male Tongan child, on turning 16 years of age, is entitled to a town allotment or property of 30 poles to build a house and a 8.25 acres of farmland to grow food for his family. This land, after it is registered in his name, is his and his descendants forever. It will pass through the oldest male child through the generations. This right is enshrined in the Tongan Constitution.

Unfortunately, now land is scarce and there are too many people so not all 16 year olds will be given land. Most families encourage their children to study hard so they can migrate and continue their studies in universities overseas and seek their fortune there. Many Tongans own property in New Zealand, Australia and the United States and other countries by purchasing them, because land can be bought and sold in those countries, including many other countries. Land in Tonga cannot be bought or sold but can be 'gifted' to relatives or any other Tongan the landowner wants to gift the land to.

The Landowner cannot 'gift' the land to anyone without 'consent' from his heirs, so it is a very safe system. For example, I cannot gift my land to anyone without consent from my heirs and family. Any member of the family can challenge any land given away by their parents or family member without good reason. The land has to be returned to the heirs because it is their constitutional and traditional right.

Heritage - Protocols

Wedding

-    A Tongan wedding is a very intense but a joyful occasion for both families. It begins with the courtship. In the old days, the young man takes his uncles and relatives with some kava and ask the girl's parents for a 'faikava'. There is usually a gift of a roast pig and yams which they share after the faikava. The young man sits next to the girl who is the 'tou'a' serving the kava. During the faikava the uncles and male relatives talk while the young man is given the opportunity to talk to the 'tou'a' or the girl. The faikava can be as long as 'all night' or whenever the young man and girl has had enough talking for one night. After several faikava, the 'couple' agrees to marry so the young man brings his uncles and relatives with a 'matapule' or talking chief and mats, tapa, a pig and some kava, on an appointed date. The kava, mats and pig are presented to the girl's family, who have assembled for the occasion, with the young man's matapule doing the talking . The girl's family matapule will reply to the presentation and 'lea mali' , as discussed in 'faka'apa'apa'.

Sometimes, at Christmas time, a Christmas card is also presented with cash that can be as much as $10,000 pa'anga (about $NZ 7,000) as a gift from the young man to the woman of his dreams. Once the families agree a date is set for the wedding and the Faifekau or Church Minister is informed. There is usually a 'fakalelea' or a night of celebrations where both families exchange gifts before the actual wedding. The Faifekau discuss the wedding protocol and maybe even several practice runs (Methodist). The Catholics usually have a kind of 'training and advisory' period for the couple with the 'Patele' or Parish Minister/Father/Padre which can be as long as 6 months.

Once the wedding day arrives there is a church ceremony with signing of the 'Marriage Certificates' by the couple, witnesses and Minister. There is usually a 'Ma'u Tohi' or Marriage Registration at the Government's Department for Registration of Birth's, Deaths and Marriages before the church ceremony. A huge feast (reception) is prepared by both families for the guests then there is also another bigger feast on the first Sunday or 'Uluaki Sapate where they wear 'Tongan Costumes' of valuable, ancient kie, ta'ovala and ngatu called the 'Tu'uvala'....after the 'uluaki Sapate....the couple are left to themselves. In many cases they already have a house built by the young man on his land of 30 poles (town allotment) and he has crops ready for harvest in his farm (8.25 acres) to feed themselves.

Deaths

- When someone dies in the family, it is a very sad occasion for all the relatives. The 'Ulumotu'a or head of the family calls a meeting of the immediate family to discuss what will be done. When all is agreed, there is an announcement or 'tala' of the death by the 'Ulumotu'a to all branches of the extended family. This is usually done by radio and a 'runner' or 'tangata fekau' will visit all the 'local' relatives to tell them ('tala') the bad news. The body of the diseased is 'prepared' by the women and is 'left in state' at the house of the oldest child or parents for 1-2 nights while the relatives come with gifts 'holo' to pay their respects to the dead. The family 'matapule' or talking chiefs 'talitali' or accept all the 'holo' which are kept in a storehouse or cooler if they are mats, tapa or slaughtered animals. The 'talitali' is usually in the same format already learned by the 'family matapule' from their predecessors.

If the 'holo' is cash...this money is given to the person already appointed to keep the cash for paying all the funeral bills. As much as $2-30,000 can be collected, depending on where the funeral is held. Overseas funerals collect more money.

Most families/relatives, who come with a 'holo'... do a 'failotu' or group prayer....with a Church Minister or Family Elder. The 'holo' goes on for the 1-2 days with the last night 'an all night singing of hymns' (Methodist) or ' 'apo fakafe'ao' to the diseased to prepare his her journey to the spirit world/heaven. It is usually referred to as the ' 'apo'. The burial is the next day with Church Ministers involved. As many as 14 Church Ministers in the

Methodist Church....can attend one burial or 'tanu'.....in the Catholic Church the burial rites is done by the 'parish priest'. In Tonga, the cemetery/ burial site are usually family owned and are prepared by the male members of the family.

There is continuous food prepared for relatives....usually light snacks and tea/coffee/cold drinks.

After the burial there is a 'feipulua' or large 'umu of food prepared for all the relatives and 'well wishers' who attended the funeral and burial. They are given a basket of food which include both rootcrop like cassava, taro, yam and meat like beef, pork, chicken. This is rarely practiced nowadays.

Most 'modern' funerals provide a 'bowl of food' for all the relatives who attend ....every night. This is practiced in Tonga and overseas as well. The funerals are usually held at a 'Funeral Home' or Church. After the burial, the 'ulumotu'a, make an announcement for everyone to go home with no further assembly for the family. That is the end of the funeral.

The Tongan funerals usually involve 'ta'one'one' or bringing sand from the beach and decoration of the 'sand mound' with flowers.

The diseased estates is usually left for the eldest and family to settle.

www.ingramcontent.com/pod-product-compliance
Lightning Source LLC
Chambersburg PA
CBHW071258130726
47998CB00003B/1238